I0776010

I hope you enjoy coloring Animal Napz and learning about the animals. Some of the patterns are inspired by textiles from the animals' home countries.

Gel pens, coloring pencils and wax crayons are the best for this paper.

Gaiatreestudio.com

What can be heard in Africa after dark?
The snoozing sounds of a sleeping aardvark.

What's that lump through the trees by the bog?
It's a big, brown bear sleeping on a log

What feels nice curled up in your lap?
A cute, little kitty cat taking a catnap.

Who's worn out after a day
full of play?
D
A pile of puppy dogs
sleeping where
they lay.

In India
you may
find another
kind of pile...
of sleepy
painted elephants
resting for a while.

What's that sound coming from the pond?
a lily lullaby ;
A froggy bedtime song.

Out on the Savanna,
curled up in a mound,
a giraffe rests her long, long neck sleeping on the ground.

Rolling around in the dirt and the mud,

Horse takes it easy, relaxing, feeling good!

neigh/snore...neigh/snore

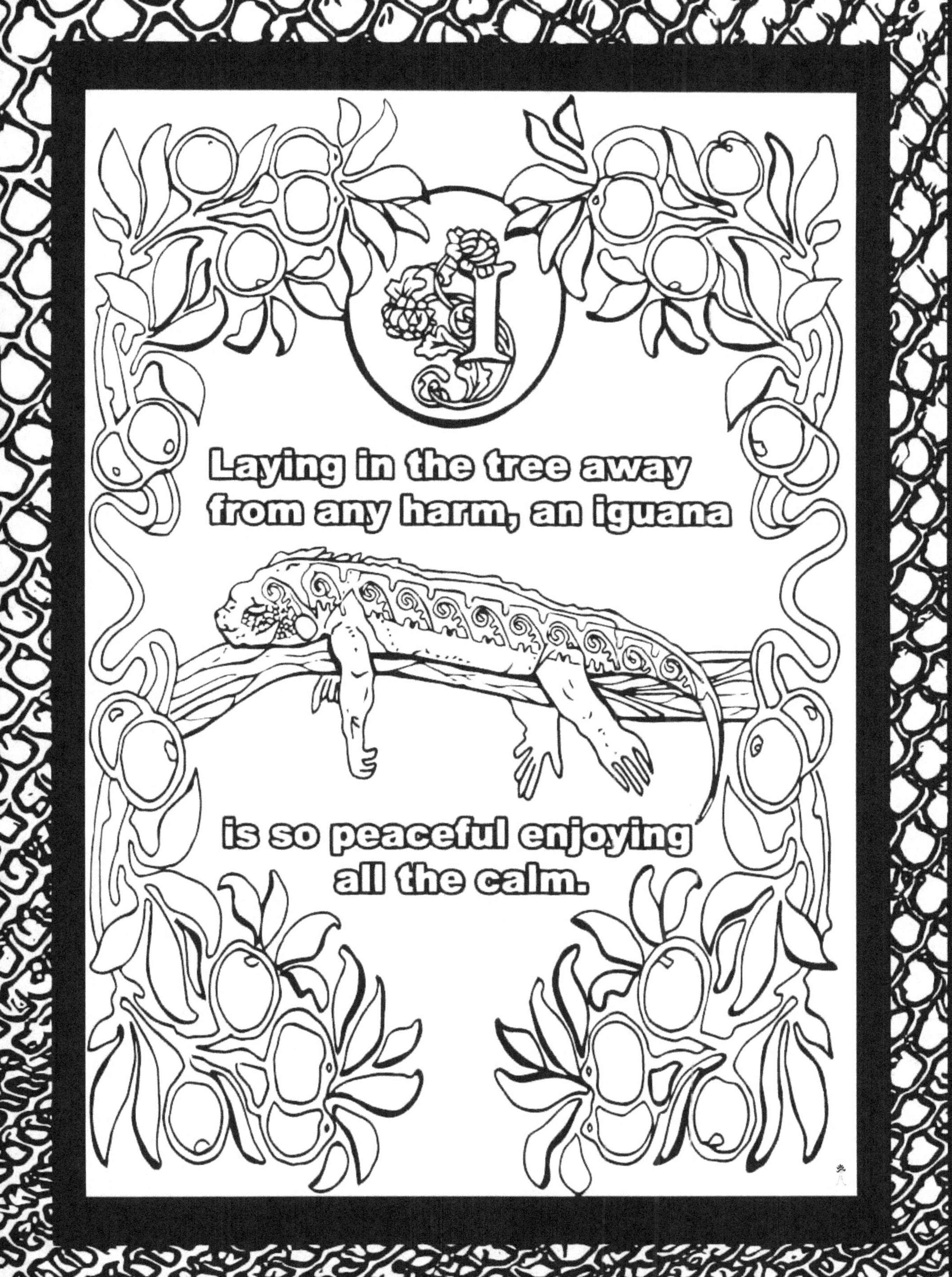

Laying in the tree away
from any harm, an iguana
is so peaceful enjoying
all the calm.

A jaguar in the jungle
hunting all night long,
needs a place to sleep when the
dark turns to dawn.

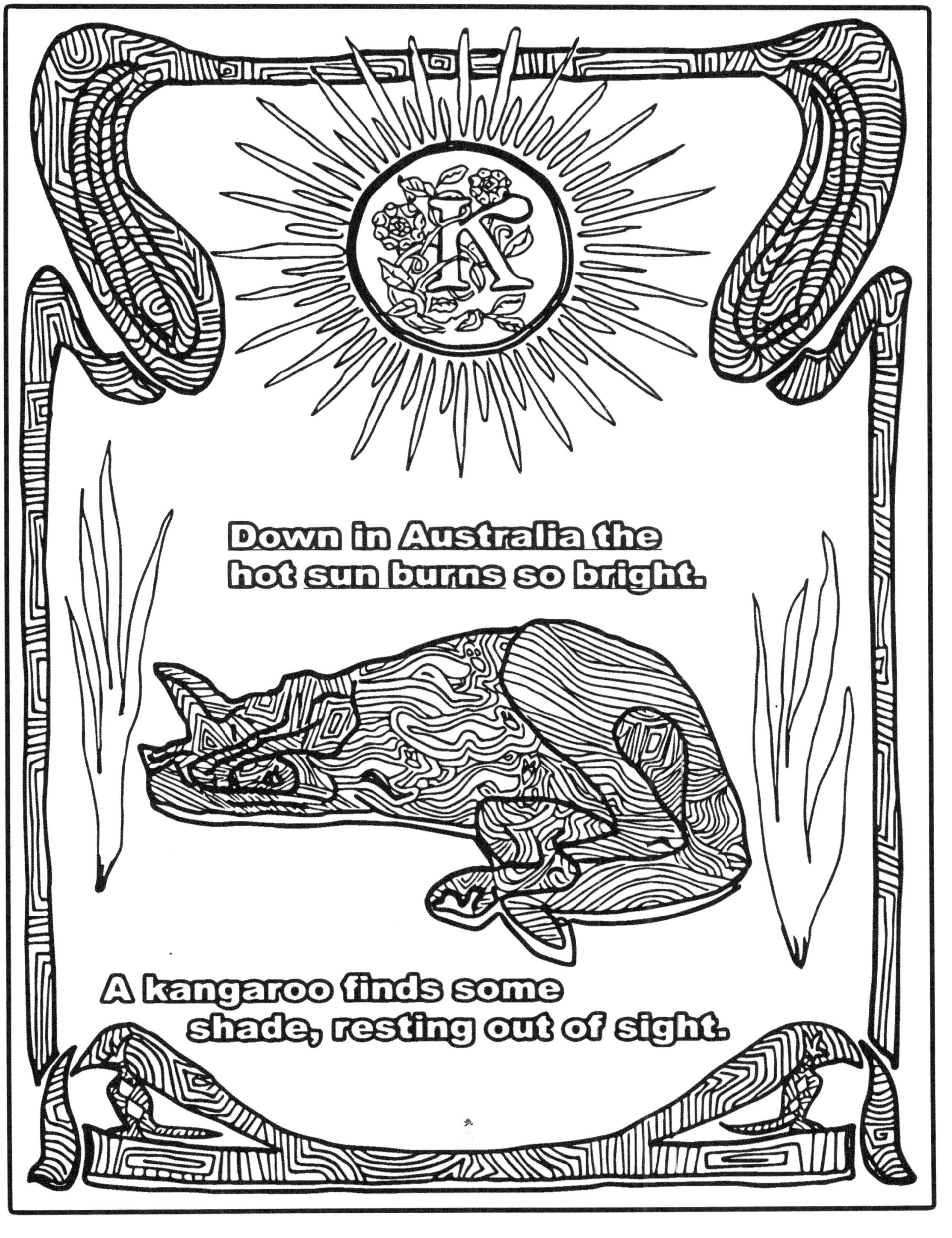

Down in Australia the
hot sun burns so bright.

A kangaroo finds some
shade, resting out of sight.

Over in Madagascar
you will find a
curious bunch
of
fuzzy ring-tailed lemurs
nappping after lunch.

Out in the country,
in the old farmhouse,

with a belly full of
cheese, there lays a
little mouse.

Ever heard of a Numbat?
She's a busy little thing...

like a stripy squirrel
who rarely stops for
napping!

Down in the town,
sleeping all the day,
an opposum in the attic comes out for moon rays.

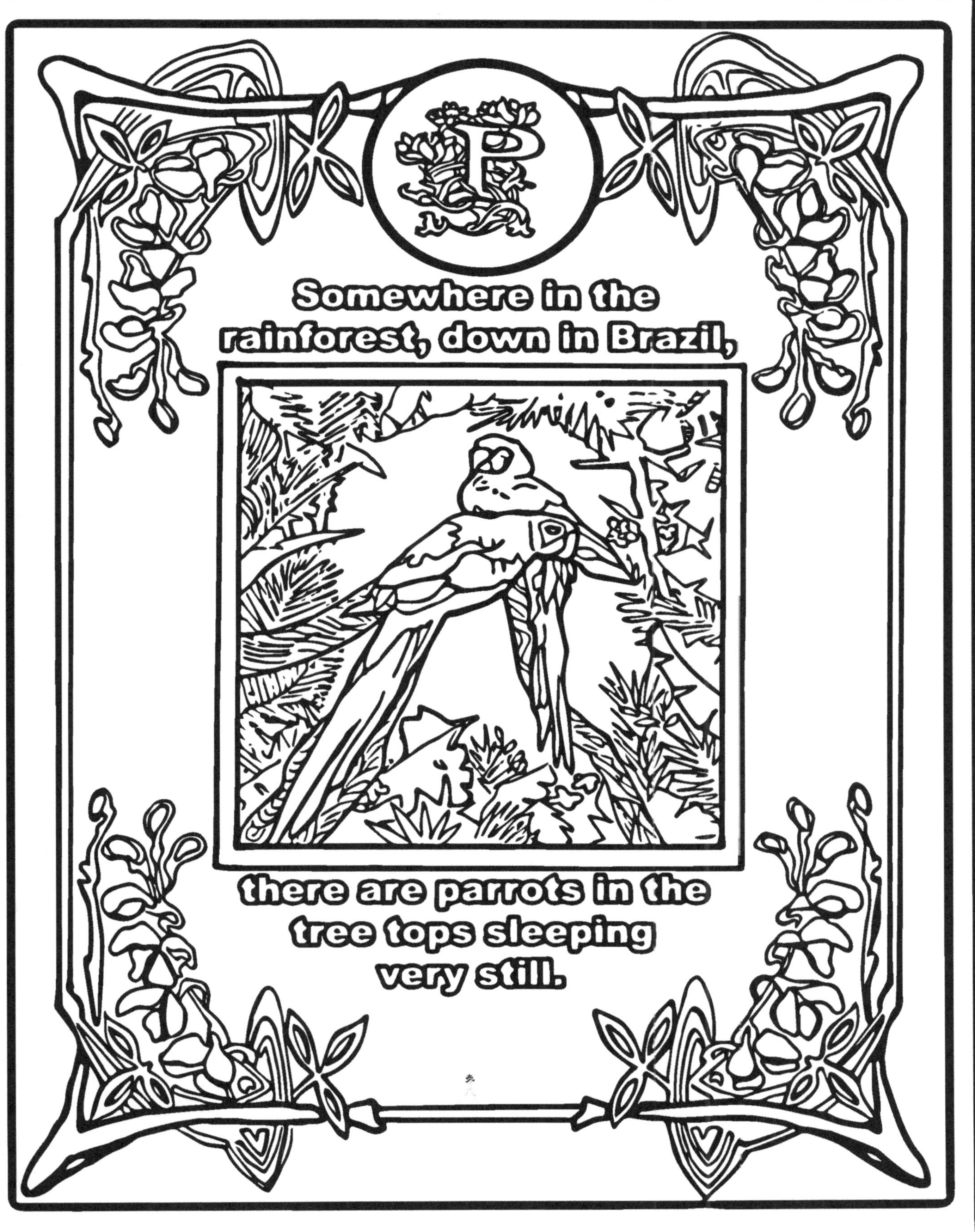

Somewhere in the rainforest, down in Brazil,
there are parrots in the tree tops sleeping very still.

What's this creature with spots on his back?
It's a quoll in New Guinea... he's got the napping knack!

A sleepy, little rabbit with a cute, cotton tail

is dreaming of carrots and yummy, green kale.

What about a snake?
How does he sleep?
Folded in a knot, tied onto the tree.

A giant tortoise thinks naps are really rather swell

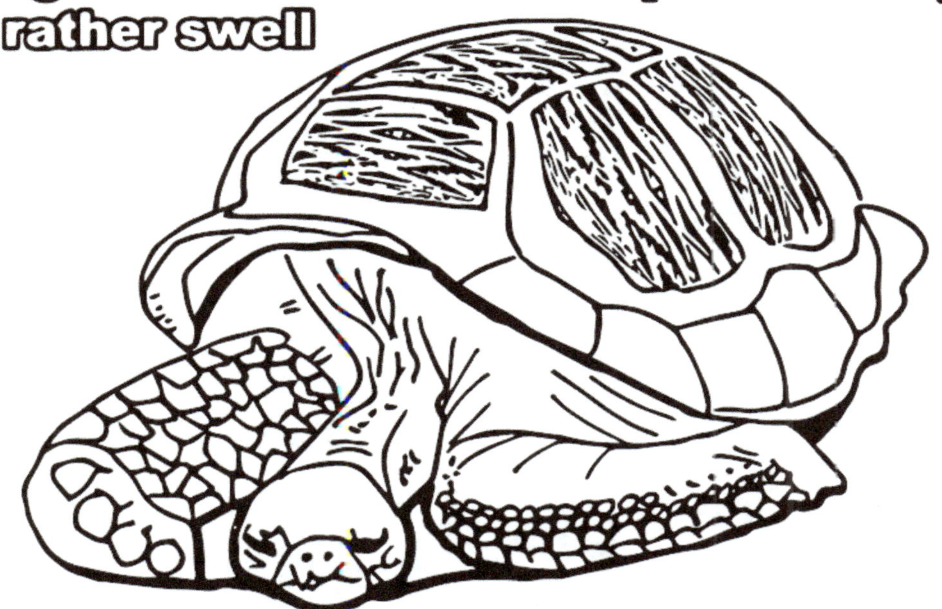

when you live so long with a big, heavy shell.

All kinds of
animals sleep up
in the trees,
including pink-faced monkeys
known as Uakaris.

Up in the Andes where the air is pure,

there's a Vicuña nodding off, can you hear her snore?

Who likes the Dreamtime
when the day is done?
A wombat in Tazmania
whose day is full of fun.

There is one little fish whose name begins with "x"...

The x-ray tetra who also likes his rest!

The very hair yak who lives in Nepal,
gets a little shut-eye
when the snow begins to fall.

How does a zebra
sleep when she
sleeps at night?

Is it in technicolor
or in black and
white?

www.ingramcontent.com/pod-product-compliance
Lightning Source LLC
Chambersburg PA
CBHW080732260726
48660CB00010B/3808